THE IMMIGRANT'S TABLE

The Immigrant's Table

LA TAVOLA DELL' IMMIGRANTE

MARY LOU SANELLI

To Karen.
Mangia!
Mary Lou

Cover art: *Boardwalk* by Lois Silver.
Courtesy of the Lisa Harris Gallery, Seattle, WA.

Author photo: Maxine Lewis Seran.

Book design and composition: Valerie Brewster, Scribe Typography.

Sanelli, Mary Lou
The Immigrant's Table / Mary Lou Sanelli
Library of Congress Control Number: 2002105940
ISBN: 1-929355-15-7

FIRST PRINTING

PUBLISHED BY

Pleasure Boat Studio: A Literary Press
201 West 89th Street, #6F
New York, NY 10024-1848

Tel/Fax: 888-810-5308
Email: pleasboat@nyc.rr.com
URL: http://www.pbstudio.com
Printed in Canada

ARTIST TRUST

IT BEGINS WITH THE ARTIST

Creation of this work was made possible in part
through a grant from Artist Trust.

For my parents:

Maria Antionette Sinsigalli

& Luigi Gabrielle Sanelli

Contents

THE RECIPES

AN INTRODUCTION

As a first-generation American and daughter of Italian immigrants who settled in the Northeast, I longed to break free of old world constraints of religion and culture both emotionally and physically. Upon arrival to the seemingly liberal west coast, I felt at ease, connected to the land and mind-set with the wide-eyed glee of a newcomer, though this sense of place lessened with the years.

As an east-coast transplant, I imitated the laid-back (a description I detest) dress and manners of my new friends. I tried to lower my voice when I spoke. To wave my hands around less. In a sense, to leave my passionate way of communicating behind, though, in spite of my efforts to conform, I hauled my upbringing around with me. As the years passed, the more I tried to leave my truest self behind, the more it snuck up to embrace me.

To reclaim who I was, I had to return home, if only through my mother's tattered recipes, to transform all I had inherited onto the page. What I found, repeatedly, was how this quest into my past triggered memories of food so bountifully at the center of our family life. And how coming of age in a home where tradition was absolute helped shape and strengthen my individual life, and, ultimately, the lives of the poems that follow.

THE IMMIGRANT'S TABLE

The Return

My mother is stunned
when I ask to borrow her recipes,
yet she senses an opportunity
lingering in my voice, that I may be grateful
for the years she relinquished to motherhood, just how little
appreciation I've shown her till now.
Presently, she accepts my lack of interest in cooking
as much as my need for solitude
and the fact I won't move back east
ever. When she hands me the stack of index cards,
flimsy from use, age, kitchen spills—no words,
just a trace of nobleness in her smile, the truth of her life
and so my own held within.

On these Pacific shores, uprooted east-coast kids
beat on drums like ancient natives, practice self-analysis
in lieu of religion. Without formality,
holidays seem like a record
played at the wrong speed, faded
as the T-shirts men wear to Christmas dinner.
And to my cautious, introverted neighbors from Minnesota,
my boisterous opinions are typically mistaken for a bite
of anger. But it is here in a newer world, I've redefined my life
and, so it seems to my family, the world.
I send poems in place of gifts

fully wrapped, bear books
instead of children.

I intend to retrace each entrée by the book,
no new-age, low-fat, vegetarian innovations. To hear what is said
when my mother's food rolls back the past on my tongue,
nothing short of transcending. Much like when I bought my home
and spent days lifting flaps of wallpaper to see who lived before.
Layer by layer, another voice dislodged
from the crumbly dark, ringing out dramatically
human as my own.

ANTIPASTO FAVORITES

Tomatoes in Oil / Pomodori all' Olio

Wash, remove stem ends and slice lengthwise

> 6 PLUM TOMATOES

Set aside.

Combine:

> 3 TABLESPOONS OLIVE OIL
> I CLOVE GARLIC, MINCED
> 3 TABLESPOONS FINELY CHOPPED BASIL
> ¼ TEASPOON OREGANO
> SALT AND PEPPER TO TASTE

Pour olive oil mixture over tomatoes and serve.

Pickled Eggplant / Melanzane con Olio e Aceto

Set out 1 quart screw-top jar.

Wash, pare and slice thin

> I EGGPLANT (APPROXIMATELY I POUND)

Put eggplant slices into jar and set aside.

Combine:

> ⅔ CUP WINE VINEGAR
> 4 CLOVES GARLIC, QUARTERED
> I GREEN PEPPER AND I RED PEPPER, SLICED

Pour mixture over eggplant and cover with

> OLIVE OIL

Screw cap onto jar and store jar in refrigerator at
least 24 hours. Serve cold.

Antipasto

Before the meal, though a meal
in and of itself. Served on Easter, Christmas.
And Thanksgiving, once the holiday was approved
by Roman-Catholics reluctant to add to their lives
celebrations not of God's making.

Salami sliced end to end, whole peppercorns
boring through pork. Prosciutto. Capocollo.
Meats difficult for our Protestant neighbors to pronounce,
meats my mother drove fifty miles away from the suburbs to buy
in the hub of the city where Italians settled
to sell cheese, shoes, lay bricks and cement.
Where my mother's sister still lived
in a narrow apartment with an Irishman, a plumber
none of us liked, and two sons
who went to parochial school
knowing work was next
not college.

A tray of provolone. Mozzarella
soft as yogurt or thick, waxy chunks
chewy as figs. Each platter of bite-sized food
flowing into the next. Olives in olive oil.
Pickled duets of eggplant and peppers.
Basil, garlic, and tiny tomatoes

Pickled Mushrooms / Funghi con Olio e Aceto

Set out 1 pint screw-top jar.

Clean but do not slice

I POUND MUSHROOMS

Place mushrooms in saucepan and cover with equal amounts of

WHITE VINEGAR AND HOT WATER

Bring mixture to boiling. Cook for five minutes. Drain liquid from mushrooms.

When mushrooms are cool, pack in jar with mixture of

¼ CUP OLIVE OIL
I TEASPOON SALT
I TEASPOON PEPPERCORNS
2 CLOVES GARLIC, HALVED

Cover mushrooms with

WHITE VINEGAR

Screw cap onto jar and store jar in refrigerator for at least 2 days before serving.

orangey-red as mercurochrome
or Aunt Connie's fingernails
pantomiming desire because she speaks
no English, each wordless gesture striking the air
rapidly, implying need, demanding her share
without sound.

MINESTRONE

Heat to boiling in a large saucepan

> 6 CUPS WATER

Wash thoroughly

> 1 GENEROUS CUP NAVY BEANS (ABOUT ½ POUND)

Gradually add beans to boiling water. Simmer 2 minutes.
Remove from heat. Set aside to soak for 1 hour.
Then add to beans

> ¼ POUND SALT PORK

Return to heat and simmer 1 hour, stirring occasionally.
Meanwhile, heat in skillet until lightly browned and set aside

> 3 TABLESPOONS OLIVE OIL
> 1 ONION, CHOPPED
> 1 CLOVE GARLIC, CHOPPED

Wash, cut into ½-inch slices and set aside

> 2 STALKS CELERY
> 2 CARROTS

Wash, pare, and dice

> 1 LARGE POTATO

Set aside.
Wash, remove outer leaves from, and shred finely

> ½ HEAD OF CABBAGE

Add all vegetables to beans with

> 1 TABLESPOON CHOPPED PARSLEY
> ½ TEASPOON SALT AND PEPPER

Minestrone

derived from the Latin "to hand out"

Aunt Josephine sets soup down
like an heirloom in front of the men
before serving the women or children.
This is our way, though we live in a country
where the opposite sequence of giving
is considered polite.

My father ferments wine in his cellar
dug into earth beneath my mother's cellar, the boiler room
with two generations of Ball jars wall-to-wall.
This is where my uncles hold refills up to the light,
compare the Chianti to their own, bottled next holiday
they host. Unquestionably, they will argue
whose *vino* is choice, adding to accusation and table pounding
all the laughter loyalty requires.

All through dinner, Cousin Johnny's date from England
looks nervous, agitated, with her cleavage exposed,
hair yellow-white as the Parmesan we heap into our bowls.
What is the matter for you? Uncle Tony asks
as if his question and our assessing stares
will help her unwind.

At our formal mahogany table
with claw-clutching-ball feet, hand-crocheted cloth

Pour in slowly

I QUART HOT WATER

Simmer 1 hour until beans are tender.

Meanwhile, cook

½ CUP WHITE RICE

About 10 minutes before beans are done, add the cooked rice and

½ CUP PEAS (FROZEN WILL DO)

Stir in

¼ CUP TOMATO PASTE

Simmer 5 minutes.

Serve sprinkled with grated Parmesan cheese.

≥ SERVES SIX ≤

draping its sides like icing,
she is the first guest to be neither family, devout,
nor willing to wait on the men
charmed by the sound of her accent.

We gape yet say nothing
when she lights a cigarette, inhaling
with a flirtatious tilt of her head, an indulgence
unallowed my mother and aunts who sneak out back to puff,
who discuss their lives in terms of aches and ailments and complain
about Cousin Johnny's girl who plays poker with the men
while the children sleep where they drop
and my aunts with faces downcast
divide and wrap what food is left.

STRACCIATELLA
Roman Egg Soup

Bring to a boil

I QUART CHICKEN BROTH

Beat until thick and piled softly

4 EGGS

Mix together well, add to eggs and beat until thoroughly combined

I TABLESPOON SEMOLINA OR WHITE FLOUR
I ½ TABLESPOON GRATED PARMESAN CHEESE
½ TEASPOON SALT
½ TEASPOON PEPPER

Slowly pour egg mixture into boiling broth, stirring continuously.

Continue stirring and simmer for 5 minutes.

Top with

CHOPPED CILANTRO OR PARSLEY

SERVES FOUR

Stracciatella

A distinct, flaky soup
lighter than Minestrone, preferable
with so much food yet to come.
Break eggs into semolina, pour into boiling broth.
Remove fat rising to the surface
luminously buoyant. Top with parsley
if cilantro can't be had.

When a bowl is served to my dad
it's at arm's length, as if my aunt waits on god the father,
afraid of the fuss he will make, the tsk
he forms with his tongue. I stare at a smudge
on her chubby hand that waves
off compliments because I don't want to see
my father's eyes rankle, the way he reluctantly tastes
any food not of his homeland
but of his in-law's province
in the part of Italy known as the boot, farther south
than he traveled before coming to America. This soup
a stretch to his allegiance.

When the aroma of pasta arrives
the mood is redeemed. Now everyone smiles.
And when the soup tureen is collected, passed high
as a baton over our heads, we pretend not to notice
my father's bowl
chock-full and sloshing the rim.

MANICOTTI

Set out two 11 × 7 × 1½ inch baking dishes.

Prepare

ITALIAN TOMATO MEAT SAUCE

When sauce is partially done, heat in skillet

2 TABLESPOONS OLIVE OIL

Add and cook until browned, breaking into small pieces with a fork

½ POUND GROUND BEEF

Remove browned beef from skillet and mix with

2 CUPS RICOTTA CHEESE
¼ POUND MOZZARELLA CHEESE, DICED
2 TABLESPOONS GRATED PARMESAN CHEESE
2 EGGS, WELL BEATEN
¾ TEASPOON SALT
¼ TEASPOON PEPPER

Set aside.

Prepare

BASIC PASTA DOUGH

Divide dough into halves. Lightly roll each half ⅛ inch thick to form
a rectangle. Cut dough lengthwise with pastry cutter into strips
5 inches wide. Cut strips every 6 inches to form noodles 5 × 6 inches.

Bring to boil

5 QUARTS WATER
I TABLESPOON SALT

Gradually add the noodles. Boil rapidly uncovered about
10 minutes or until noodles are tender.

Manicotti

When at last it is served, tubes
like thick white fingers
bubbling in parmigiano, pungent wedge
liberally grated, no one is hungry.
Still, pasta is the ceremonial heart of the meal.
Our plates must swim in it.

The men with faces round, chests round, waists round,
loosen their belts, slap their sides, make a show
of whose belly rolls soft and widest.

My sister refuses the ricotta-filled feast,
nurses her hunger with celery, unbuttered bread.
As an entrant in the Knights of Columbus Beauty Pageant,
dieting is practice for the event
as much as leg lifts, sit ups, walking in her satin gown
up and down the stairs in heels. And a deep-seated fear
that in the end, no matter what talent she hones,
grade-point-average she carries, or world-view response
she manages to articulate with poise, all that will count
for a thing is the swim suit competition.

Broad, oval platters
heaped with browned beef and pork.
Artichoke leaves spread and stuffed.

Drain by pouring into a colander.

Lay noodles out on a flat surface. About ½ inch from the lengthwise edge of the noodle, place 4 tablespoons of filling. Spread the filling from narrow edge to narrow edge so filling is in a ½ inch wide mound. Roll the ½ inch edge of dough over the filling and continue to roll. Press edges to seal. Place 4 to 6 manicotti into each baking dish in a single layer. Cover with Tomato Meat Sauce.

Bake at 400° F about 20 minutes or until tomato sauce is bubbling hot and manicotti swell.

Serve with remaining meat sauce.

➤ ABOUT EIGHT SERVINGS ◄

Insalata of endive, escarole, romaine.
Cores cut out, served after the meal. Not before.
Extra helpings saved for my sister
whose will to be thin
none of us can chide away.

GNOCCHI

Wash, pare and cook covered in boiling, salted water

3 LARGE POTATOES, CUT IN QUARTERS

Cook about 20 minutes or until tender. Drain.

Mash potatoes, keep hot.

Measure into bowl

1¾ CUPS SIFTED FLOUR

Make a well in center of flour. Add mashed potatoes.

Mix well to make a soft, elastic dough. Turn dough onto a lightly floured surface and knead.

Break off small pieces of dough and use palm of hand to roll pieces to pencil thickness. Cut into pieces about ¾ inches long. Curl each piece by pressing lightly with the index finger and pulling the finger along the piece of dough toward you. Gnocchi may also be shaped by pressing each piece lightly with a floured fork.

Bring to boil in a saucepan

3 QUARTS WATER

Gradually add the gnocchi. Boil rapidly uncovered about 10 minutes or until gnocchi come to the surface. Drain by pouring into a colander.

Top with Tomato Meat Sauce.

❧ ABOUT SIX SERVINGS ❧

Gnocchi

Scallop the edges
so each gnocchi is a small potato pie.
Press lightly with a cold fork. Tender as butter,
prongs slip right through.

Surnamed Sinsigalli, married to Sanelli,
you might imagine my mother at home
in the aisles of the A & P where she loads two carts
to overflowing, six dozen eggs stacked in the child's seat,
sacks of flour heaped like sandbags against the rain.
I'm mortified when she asks two strangers to help
roll the weight of my family's appetite to checkout.

If Dad reeks aftershave
company is coming. I polish his shoes church-bright.
Mom stops shouting when the house is transformed
to where tidy people live.

When Uncle Pete pulls up in a pearl-white Cadillac
that leaks dark drops of oil on our weedless lawn,
my new aunt sits beside him
just off the boat, a greenhorn, my father says
in a voice sharp-edged, superior.
To me, she looks like the hippy-kids at school
in heelless sandals, thick wool socks

coiled under an ankle-length skirt, hair tied back
with a floral scarf, legs hairy as grassland. The same kids
my father calls lazy, despising all those born into money,
the way they shrug it. Their idleness an affront
to his ruthless way of work, work, work,
work, work.

My mother reaches out, open-palmed,
walks my aunt to the kitchen where they drop
spoons full of dough into boiling water.

When I think of that day,
whatever came after the meal: cigar smoke, poker played...
my aunt from the old country is what I like to recall.
The way she pinched my cheek, cupped my face, called me
bella, bella.

BASIC PASTA DOUGH

Sift into a large bowl a mixture of

4 CUPS SIFTED FLOUR
½ TEASPOON SALT

Make a well in center of flour. Add, one at a time, mixing slightly after each addition

4 EGGS

Add gradually

6 TABLESPOONS COLD WATER

Mix well to make a stiff dough. Turn dough onto a lightly floured surface and knead.

To make Pasta Verde, (green noodles) mix well into the dough after eggs are added

¼ POUND COOKED, FINELY CHOPPED SPINACH

Basic Pasta Creed

Linguine, vermicelli, ravioli, manicotti.
Strings, shells, squares, tubes.
For color, add spinach to the last layer of dough.

Do not over-boil, each noodle mushy, bending
like a blade of grass till it severs, but al dente,
texture firmly pliable, ample as meat.

In the warm cradle of my mother's arms,
I was spoon fed orzo, rice-sized semolina
heated with milk and mashed with fruit. Each morning
I must have stared deep into the lingering shadows
of her presence, clothed and scented, her brunette eyes
and frizzy dark hair, the dip between her breasts, her mouth
opening and closing with the latest Sinatra song. Felt her pulse
beating through her fingers as I grabbed for another mouthful
before it wriggled through my lips to slide
perfectly down.

From then on, pasta at the epicenter
of my well-groomed existence.
Monday, Wednesday, Friday, Sunday,
helpings served lottery-size.
Tuesday, Thursday, Saturday,
spaghetti as a side dish, but not a vestige,

ITALIAN TOMATO MEAT SAUCE
Salsa di Carne al Pomodoro

Set out a large sauce pot having a tight-fitting cover.

Heat in sauce pot

> ¼ CUP OLIVE OIL

Add and cook until lightly browned

> I MEDIUM CHOPPED ONION

Add and brown, turning occasionally

> ½ POUND GROUND BEEF CHUCK
> ½ POUND GROUND PORK SHOULDER
> (OR SUBSTITUTE I POUND OF GROUND BEEF)

Add slowly a mixture of

> 7 CUPS OF SIEVED, CANNED TOMATOES
> I TABLESPOON SALT
> I BAY LEAF

Cover sauce pot and simmer over very low heat, about 2½ hours.

Add

> ¾ CUP (6 OZ. CAN) TOMATO PASTE

Simmer uncovered over very low heat, stirring occasionally,
about two hours or until thickened. Remove bay leaf from sauce.
Serve over cooked pasta.

➤ ABOUT FOUR CUPS OF SAUCE ◄

accompanying chicken or chops, the way nails
belong at the end of your hand.

Now inborn roots reach deeper
than will can go. I know from experience
it's no use denying. When the voice inside me commands
starch and carbohydrate, I comply.
I tell you this because Catholics need to confess:
Nothing else is complete food.
Nothing else completely feeds me.

Finocchio

Plates of anise-seasoned fennel
passed between sighs, our stomachs expanding
and presently this moment
the room is silent.

Each crisp, aromatic stalk
cleans the palate between courses.
Before more wine is poured and tomato sauce
streams down our chins.

On Christmas Eve, in starched crinolines
and collars, we sit at the table at five.
Stay seated till nine or ten
until cappuccino is warm in our hands,
appetite a stone we've kicked aside.

In the kitchen
my mother, endorphin driven, consumed
by all there is to do, sings show tunes
off key, wipes each surface till stainless shines
as mirrors do. This is how, I understand
years later when I am more like her than I thought,
she summoned passion into her life. Music
a creative foothold by which she could stand
in the stifling order of things, quietly

fearful compliments from her family
might not come to pass
because she needs them so much.

Pig's Feet

Under the chandelier my mother cherishes,
we cross ourselves, join forehead to heart and breasts
with a jab of the thumb.

When the meat is passed, my sister spears a pig's foot
from a thick of tomatoes, a fatty chunk of claw
that looks as if it is not for eating, should never be eaten
but it is the prize of our sauce more than sausage
firm in its sheath or meatballs packed into roundness
in the palm of my mother's hand.

I'm fifteen and no longer buy the Virgin Mary.
If true, why only the son of God?
Why doesn't Mary get credit?
My father's voice shifts to reprimand close to disgust
in his eyes. I question everything my parents stand for
and they won't stand for it. Unallowed to eat
I'm sent to my room.

Later, my godfather tucks my flat-chested self
under his arm, leads me to the kitchen
where leftovers are packed into cartons
evenly spaced as church pews. This is how a feast ends up
when no one is left to feed. I sulk, elbows on the table,
hands pressed against my cheeks, temper eased.

He makes me a plate, makes me laugh,
pulls a pig's foot from his pocket, wax-papered,
saved on the sly. Until this day, ignoring my father's punishment
is a behavior in our home
beyond imagining.

My godfather speaks candid English, is college-educated.
In his presence, my father acquiesces, patrols us
but does not interfere. In the dining room, the men all talk
at once, embellishing stories with pounding fists
and hearts as I sit smiling into my knuckles of pork,
gristly toes and greasy skin, unrefined
as the organs we like to eat.

PROSCIUTTO AND MELON
Antipasto di Prosciutto e Melone

The contrasting flavors of ham and subtle melon combine in this simple appetizer.

Wash, cut into halves, and remove seeds from center

I CANTALOUPE, CHILLED

Cube each cantaloupe half into 1 inch pieces.

Wrap around each cube of cantaloupe and secure with a wooden toothpick

THIN SLICES OF PROSCIUTTO

Serve immediately.

Prosciutto and Melon

From the south side of our home
full views of a swimming pool my father installed
though he never learned to swim. Clearly,
the vinyl-lined oval of blue makes Cousin Marie uneasy—
all the bricks her husband lays will never amount
to our family's success: our leaving the city for suburbs.
When she visits with her muscular husband, the goombah
who knows no English, my father creeps like sun
across a field to his den, retreats to his recliner, shields himself,
a blind between in-laws so taut it denies entry.

At the sink, my mother talks ceaselessly
as crows do when food is near, wraps prosciutto
around tiny scoops of cantaloupe, a soft coupling
of meat to fruit. I learn my grandmother chewed tobacco,
my grandfather bootlegged beer. But what sneaks up
like a crook from behind is hearing my mother quit high school
to roll long loaves of crusty pane, its aroma
seducing passers-by who taste the yeasty air and fall
under its womb-like spell—and to grind sausage,
cranking a metal handle to slip pork free of bone,
the weight of casings hung in the wine cellar
link by link.

In a kitchen thick with garlic, wreathed in steam,
women prepare food, remember food.
Deep hungers for memory rise from their breasts
like rowdy laughter, thicken ties between them

while two men with minds
under wraps, sit in full-bodied coats
of armor, denying the past they share, the present.
No noise but the halts and starts of a television, John Wayne
perched within reach. No part of either man
willing to dilate, to open and enter the place
where the other can afford to live.

VEAL SCALOPPINE
Scaloppine di Vitello

Set out a large, heavy skillet having a tight-fitting cover.

Place meat on flat working surface and repeatedly pound (to increase the meats tenderness) meat on one side with a meat hammer, turn and repeat process on other side

> I POUND VEAL ROUND STEAK (CUTLET) CUT ABOUT
> ½ INCH THICK

Cut veal into 1 inch pieces. To coat veal evenly, shake 2 pieces at a time in a plastic bag containing a mixture of

> ½ CUP FLOUR
> ½ TEASPOON OREGANO
> ½ TEASPOON SALT
> ⅛ TEASPOON PEPPER

Set aside.

Heat in skillet until garlic is lightly browned

> I LARGE CLOVE OF GARLIC, SLICED THIN
> ¼ CUP OLIVE OIL

Add veal to garlic and olive oil and slowly brown on both sides.

While veal is browning, combine

> I ¾ CUPS STEWED TOMATOES
> ½ TEASPOON SALT
> ½ TEASPOON CHOPPED CILANTRO (OR PARSLEY)
> ⅛ TEASPOON PEPPER

Slowly add tomato mixture to browned veal.

Cover skillet and simmer about 30 minutes or until veal is tender. If mixture becomes too thick, add a small amount of water.

⮑ ABOUT FOUR SERVINGS ⮐

Veal Scaloppine

On the counter I leave pictures of calves
crammed into metal cages, heads protruding,
constricted between bars of steel, eyes bulging
in wide balls of fear. My mother's pity wells up,
torments, but still she pounds with a blunt wooden mallet
until each cutlet is tender, veins and capillaries
crushed into submission.

I am sixteen, reborn vegetarian, enraged
at my meat-eating family, the beef-eating world.
I scream that her cooking is cruel, sadistic.
This is when she yells for my father, the sound of his feet
ponderous on the stairs.

I lock my door, turn up The Temptations, refuse
to respond to scolding until my bravado resigns
gutlessly into tears, the pressure between my ears
released by his disapproval. Even now,
with the hair at my temples turning white
as strands of cotton, if I take my parents on
it comes to this. Composure washed away.
Streaks of mascara running down my cheeks.

Until, say, a year later I relent, laughing
at last more than crying. When served Scaloppine,

CHICKEN CACCIATORE
Pollo alla Cacciatore

Heat in a large, heavy skillet until garlic is lightly browned

> ½ CUP OLIVE OIL
> 2 CLOVES GARLIC, SLICED THIN

Meanwhile, prepare and coat with flour mixture of

> ½ CUP OF FLOUR AND 1 TEASPOON SALT
> 1 FRYING CHICKEN, 2 TO 3 POUNDS

Place chicken skin-side down in skillet containing oil and garlic.

Turn as necessary to brown all sides.

Combine

> 3½ CUPS TOMATOES, SIEVED
> 1 TEASPOON SALT
> 1 TEASPOON OREGANO
> ½ TEASPOON PEPPER
> 1 TEASPOON CHOPPED PARSLEY

Slowly add tomato mixture to browned chicken.

Cook slowly 30 minutes or until meatiest pieces of chicken are tender when pierced with a fork.

If mixture becomes too thick, add a small amount of water.

⮞ ABOUT FOUR SERVINGS ⮜

veal smothered in bisque, I feast, quietly, on bread.
Or *Cacciatore*, tomatoes above
and on either side of chicken, I dine on bread,
righteous in my newly found tolerance,
my parent's lives handed to me
calmly. My first understanding of how I could be
completely with them, for them, of them
but not them.

POLENTA

Cut casing, remove sausage and crumble it into
small pieces

I POUND ITALIAN SAUSAGE

Clean and slice

I POUND MUSHROOMS

Heat in skillet

2 TABLESPOONS OLIVE OIL

Add mushrooms and sausage to skillet. Cook slowly,
stirring occasionally, until mushrooms and sausage
are lightly browned.

Slowly stir in a mixture of

2½ CUPS CANNED TOMATOES
I TEASPOON SALT
½ TEASPOON PEPPER

Simmer 25 to 30 minutes.

Meanwhile, bring to boiling in a saucepan

3 CUPS WATER
I½ TEASPOON SALT

Gradually stir in a mixture of

I CUP YELLOW CORN MEAL
I CUP COLD WATER

Continue boiling, stirring constantly, until mixture
is thickened.

Cover, lower heat, and cook slowly 10 minutes.

Polenta

On the Friday before Lent,
people of Ponti, Italy, celebrate the feast of Polentine.
After a parade to honor corn,
huge helpings fried into cakes soaked
with compassion are served to the poor.

I add sausage to the skillet. A fist full of herbs
fresh picked today, just now.

When asked about the smooth, quarter-moon scar
branding the side of my thumb, I say
with a stage sense of knowing
when to make people laugh
freeing crust from the fiery hold of cast iron
is tougher than it looks.

I try to hide the blister
swelling two-ply from my skin
as I set heaps of charred, crumbled polenta
on the one place not yet covered with food.

My family, seated around a sprawl of platters, is tied
to umbilical bonds linking carbohydrates to pleasure.
Their appreciation of my effort takes up the room
between our worlds. They release *ahh* from their throats
as if my offering is intact, fluffy and fit to display.

Transfer cooked corn meal to a warm platter and top with tomato mixture.

Sprinkle with

GRATED PARMESAN OR ROMANO CHEESE

Serve immediately.

➤ SIX TO EIGHT SERVINGS ◀

Aunt Josephine throws her head back and claps,
spreads both palms and lifts her plump arms
to frame her luscious breasts
like a woman in a biblical painting.
She is relieved I've worn
out my disinterest in food, that the faraway niece
who shuns tradition and cares nothing for cooking,
finally comes home
to cook.

SALADS

Red Kidney Bean Salad / Insalata di Fagioli

Drain

> 2 CUPS OF CANNED KIDNEY BEANS

Combine beans with mixture of

> ¼ CUP WINE VINEGAR
> 3 TABLESPOONS OLIVE OIL
> ¼ TEASPOON OREGANO
> ¼ TEASPOON SALT AND PEPPER

Blend in

> ¼ CUP DICED CELERY
> 2 TABLESPOONS CHOPPED ONION

Place in refrigerator. Chill. Serve in crisp lettuce cups.

➢ FOUR SERVINGS ➢

Insalata Verde / Green Salad

Wash in cold water equal amounts of salad greens

> CURLY ENDIVE
> ROMAINE
> SMALL DANDELION GREENS
> ESCAROLE OR CHICORY

Drain, dry thoroughly and carefully tear (never cut) lettuce in bite-size pieces.

Pizzelle on the Fourth of July

Three generations seated around a picnic table
in shorts, gauzy shirts. If not for our gold chains, dark hair
and skin, pot-bellies that circle our backs and calves
round as melons, the yard could be an ad for healthy living.

A connected circle of hands, heads bowed, grace given
with the sign of the cross, a poke to the bridge of the nose,
breastbone, chest left to right. Now eating springs free
as we make a religion out of food, attack our plates
with the weight of summer salad: pasta, potato, bean, fruit.
A coveted bowl of dandelion greens I'm paid to pick,
working my thumb between grass and stem before bitter sets in.

When my mother's fashionable friend arrives
taller, richer, more educated than any man here,
my father sits stiffly, masks his insecurity with smugness.
All he dislikes about his WASP neighbors is visible
in his self-consciousness: men with manicured hands,
women who achieve outside the boundaries of home.
When she unwraps her chicken, a potent smell wafts up.
My mother and aunt eye each other, move to a command
inaudible to us, circle the pan like contestants on a wrestling mat.
Later, my mother will walk our neighbor home, explain

Chill in sealed plastic bag or covered bowl in refrigerator 1 hour.

Just before serving, rub a wooden bowl with

I CLOVE GARLIC, CUT IN HALF

Put greens into bowl and pour over

6 TABLESPOONS ITALIAN DRESSING
(SEE NEXT RECIPE)

Using a salad spoon and fork, turn and toss the greens until well coated with dressing and no liquid remains on bottom of bowl.

≥ ABOUT SIX SERVINGS ≤

Italian Dressing

Combine in a screw-top jar

6 TABLESPOONS EXTRA VIRGIN OLIVE OIL
3 TABLESPOONS WINE VINEGAR
I CLOVE GARLIC, CRUSHED
¼ TEASPOON SALT
⅛ TEASPOON PEPPER
2 ANCHOVY FILLETS, FINELY CHOPPED
(OPTIONAL)

Shake well. Chill in refrigerator. Shake thoroughly before serving.

≥ ABOUT ½ CUP OF DRESSING ≤

without shifting her smile, that Greek olive oil is too gamy
to fry in, no substitute for Italian
while drums, wings, and thighs
sway side-to-side in her friend's foil pan.

Now, guests gone, my mother and I press Pizzelle,
thick yellow batter poured onto iron grids. In the morning
in our church basement, orderly as the confessionals overhead,
we gather after mass to share our pyramid of wafers
fragile as glass. After we mouth our hymns, drop coins
into an assertive basket, and incense clouds the aisles till we cough
and my father curses out loud. Then, on to the cemetery
to ornament our graves like nosegays.

That summer so many reasons to spend time
with my mother. I was seventeen. So much to mend
before entering a future I secretly feared,
one without the other in it, made more real
by our inability to speak of it.

PANE
Italian Bread

Lightly grease 15½ × 12 inch baking sheet.

Soften

    I PACKAGE ACTIVE DRY YEAST IN ¼ CUP WARM WATER

Let stand 5 to 10 minutes.

Meanwhile, put into a large bowl

    I ¾ CUPS WARM WATER
    I TABLESPOON SALT

Blend in

    3 CUPS SIFTED FLOUR

Stir softened yeast, and add to flour-water mixture, mixing well.

Measure

    2 ½ CUPS SIFTED FLOUR

Add about one-half the flour to the yeast mixture and beat until very smooth. Mix in enough remaining flour to make a soft dough. Turn mixture onto a lightly floured surface.

Allow to stand for 10 minutes. Knead.

Select a deep bowl large enough to allow dough to double. Shape dough into a smooth ball and place in greased bowl. Turn dough until greased surface in on top. Cover bowl with waxed paper and towel and let stand in warm place until dough is doubled (about 1½ hours).

Punch down with fist. Knead on a lightly floured surface, about 2 minutes. Divide into two equal balls. Let stand covered 10 minutes.

Roll each ball of dough into a 14 × 8 inch rectangle. Roll up tightly into a long, slender loaf.

Sliced Meat
and Bread

I take a stand against Vietnam but nothing I say
sways my father. Secretly I know
I know nothing of war, but my temper is flung against his.
He loosens his belt. Counts to ten. I'm sobbing
by the time he says *cinque*. From another room,
my mother pleads with the whole of my name
plus the one tacked on at Confirmation,
our Catholic coming of age: *Maria Louisa Gabriella,*
for the love of God, let us eat in peace!
before she repeats the words
softly, whispering her plea into two folded hands
as if it were prayer.

Now, under the weight of her distress, its residue
echoing off our kitchen walls, we spread the table.
My mother throwing her anger into it, bosom heaving
as cheese is cut from tire-sized wheels, bread from loaves
long as my arm. Meat sliced thin as cellophane.
Suddenly, as if on tip-toe, my fit shrivels, is gone.

We finish with fruit, rinds carved free, a family
of knives working rhythmically as the second
hand on a watch. This is when my father stands, grinning

Pinch ends to seal. Place loaves on prepared baking sheet. Cover loaves loosely with a towel and set aside in a warm place until doubled.

Bake at 425° F 10 minutes. Reduce temperature to 350° and bake 1 hour, or until golden brown.

To increase crustiness cherished by the Italians, place a flat pan on bottom of oven and fill with boiling water at beginning of baking period.

➤ MAKES TWO LOAVES ◄

like an M.C. before walking to the den where he will read
from a book that opens his memories of war
like a scalpel. The war. Hitler's. Mussolini's
men who made camp on his family farm.
My father revealing his past with words
that permeate my childhood like his cigarette smoke.
He says everything to eat, the army ate.
Everything of value, stolen. Furniture, clothes, books
burned to keep soldiers warm. In so much cold

and fear, my father trudged the land
for berries and squirrels to skin, his cache
bedded in straw. His mother so thin, so scared.
His sister sleeping on floorboards in a corner of the goat barn,
her breath steaming, rising
to be part of the air.

PASTA FAGIOLI
Pasta with Beans

Heat to boiling in a large saucepan

> 3 CUPS WATER

Gradually add

> 1 ¼ CUPS NAVY BEANS

to water so boiling will not stop. Simmer 2 minutes and remove from heat.

Set aside to soak for 1 hour.

Add to beans

> ½ TEASPOON SALT

Return to heat and simmer 2 hours until beans are tender.

Meanwhile, heat to boiling in large saucepan

> 2 QUARTS WATER
> 1 TEASPOON SALT

Gradually add

> 2 CUPS DITALINI

Boil rapidly uncovered about 12 minutes or until ditalini is tender. Reserving

1 cup liquid, drain ditalini by pouring into a colander. When beans are tender, add drained ditalini, the 1 cup of reserved liquid, and a mixture of

> ¼ CUP TOMATOES, SIEVED
> 1 TABLESPOON OLIVE OIL
> ¼ TEASPOON PEPPER
> ½ TEASPOON OREGANO

Pasta Fagioli

I like to visit the desert in a heat-wave,
locals tucked inside, curtains drawn till dusk.
When I walk into the wavering air
and a mourning dove sings her melancholy notes,
I close my eyes and lean my head against the nearest rail.
Anyone seeing me might think I'm ill, but it's only my past
rousing till I feel it in my knees. No other sound
triggers my biology so intensely, though I grew up in New England.
Wrong weather. No dove cooed our suburban 'scape.

Now, sitting here by the Pacific, who knows why my memory
suddenly widens like sun, out for its moment, crossing the sound.
And I remember Friday evenings, Dad on the couch, mud-covered
boots left by the door. In the kitchen, a week's leftovers
mixed with chicken-broth, any greens starting to turn.
The soup rips in a pressure cooker or slow-seasons in terra-cotta
hinging on whether our father is dozing or fully asleep
and we are scolded for any sounds we make
until he wipes the last fagioli from his bowl,
bread crust crumbling in his grip.

Then, my first kiss
behind the garage where corn grows lofty
as adolescent desire. A boy's tongue enters my mouth,
his pulse beats between my teeth. Aroused, I pull away,

Simmer 10 to 15 minutes. Serve sprinkled with

GRATED PARMESAN CHEESE

Serve immediately.

⋑ ABOUT FIVE SERVINGS ⋐

my clumsy, underdeveloped body falling into stalks that snap
like kindling. I fear Father Angelo's condemnation, the back
of my father's hand, heckling in school when word gets out.

Moving on to Christmas Eve. Anticipation so possessed
I ache with it. The house hysterical, trimmed gaudy, raucous
with lights. In my adult life, I find recreating this degree of joy
unobtainable though I buy the gifts and food: seven kinds
of smelly fish staring from the fridge.

Over us, a portrait of my grandfather
standing on a hidden box to be tall
as his black-veiled wife, arranged marriage, photograph shot
torso up. An elaborate, gold-plated frame draped in rosary beads
like tiny black olives strung on our dining room wall.
Each meal served so the dead will see.

EASTER EGG BREAD
Pane de Pasqua all' Uovo

Lightly butter 15½ × 12 inch baking sheet.

Color (follow directions on food dye) and set aside

> 5 UNCOOKED EGGS

Soften

> 2 PACKAGES ACTIVE DRY YEAST IN ½ CUP WARM WATER

Let stand 5 to 10 minutes.

Meanwhile, pour into a large bowl

> ½ CUP WARM WATER

Blend in

> 1½ CUPS SIFTED FLOUR

Stir yeast, add to flour-water mixture. Beat until very smooth.

Cover bowl with waxed paper and towel and let stand in warm place for 1½ to 2 hours.

Cream until softened

> ¾ CUP SHORTENING
> 2 TABLESPOONS LEMON JUICE
> 1 TABLESPOON GRATED LEMON PEEL

Add gradually, creaming until fluffy after each addition, a mixture of

> 1 CUP SUGAR
> 1 TEASPOON SALT

Beat until thick and piled softly

> 2 EGGS
> 1 EGG WHITE

Pane di Pasqua
all' Uovo

Vigorously, my mother kneads the dough,
punching with one fist, then both fists.
Flour dusts her feet. White tracks
by the sink, refrigerator, phone.

A damp cloth covers three milk-white balls.
When they have doubled, swollen like bellies,
she rolls each into equal lengths to braid,
her new friend saying she can't believe
how much preparation Eyetalian holidays take.
We flinch because there is no good way
to deny or correct this misuse of sound
light-years from appropriate.

In a snowed-in cul-de-sac,
Protestant, Methodist, and atheist women
walk knee-deep in snowdrifts to our home
to be buoyed by homespun wreaths
of warm bread, peppermint-sweet,
dotted with six shades of eggs.

Before they come, I watch my mother stand
on a chair to remove the crucifix from our kitchen wall.

Add beaten eggs in thirds to sugar mixture, beating thoroughly after each addition.

Add yeast mixture, mixing well.

Measure

4½ CUPS SIFTED FLOUR

Add about one-half of the flour to yeast mixture and beat until smooth. Mix in enough flour to make a soft dough. Knead on a lightly floured surface.

Select a deep bowl large enough to allow dough to double. Shape dough into a smooth ball and place into greased bowl. Turn dough until greased surface in on top. Cover bowl with waxed paper and towel and let dough rise until doubled (about 1½ hours).

Punch down with fist. Divide dough into two equal balls. Let stand covered for 10 minutes.

Roll each ball out into a long roll about 35 inches long and one inch thick. Using the two long pieces of dough, form a loosely braided ring, leaving spaces for the five colored eggs. Place on prepared baking sheet. Place colored eggs into spaces of braid. Cover loosely with towel.

Set aside in a warm place until doubled.

Bake at 350° F for 10 minutes.

Brush bread with a mixture of

I EGG YOLK AND I TABLESPOON MILK

Bake 40 to 45 minutes until bread is golden brown. Eggs will be hard-cooked.

Our neighbors sit around the table, admiring.
Since moving from Little Italy to the suburbs
this is what my mother craves, to be unique,
not provincial in their minds.

FRUTTA
Fruit Plate

Chill large serving plate.

Cut into halves

4 CHILLED PEACHES

Wash and chill

½ POUND RED GRAPES
½ POUND GREEN GRAPES

Arrange peach halves in the center of the serving plate.

Pare and cut each into 6 wedges

½ CHILLED CANTALOUPE
½ CHILLED HONEYDEW MELON

Core, peel, and cut into wedges

4 CHILLED APPLES

Arrange all fruit wedges around peaches on plate.

Place small clusters of grapes between melon wedges.

Garnish with

MINT LEAVES

Serve immediately.

Frutta

Hold an apple in your palm
firmly as your grandmother's knickknack.
Polish until it shines like her linoleum.
Pare in one continual spiral, underside down.
Cut pulp from core. Slice to hold a slab of Gorgonzola,
green-veined as skin, lean as silk.
In your other hand, figs or pomegranate
staining red.

Between *grappa* to come and the last fruit to go
we wait, though at this pace it's more of a pause
before *espresso* is served with *Sambuca*,
licorice liqueur we sip with serious eating behind us
a couple of courses ago.

When the women stand to clear it is too much
for me to imagine myself staging such a meal.
The uncles stare but stay seated, oblivious to all
but cigars clenched between their teeth, poker chips
restless in their hands.

In my rebellious teenage mind, red flashes,
nerves ignite, tiny infernos give way to will.
I try to adjust my family's alignment. In a voice
thunderous without volume

I ask the men to help! I am a minnow
challenging a sea of King Salmon
and though they pretend not to hear
they watch my every move. In the size of their disapproval
I will live a lifetime.

With my head down, I stack each plate where I am
closest to my mother, her arms laden with platters,
each bowl perched perilously as the scorn
she extends to my father. The unspoken between them
I heed the way a dog hears a mute whistle, the acute silence
before shouting devours us.

Chestnuts

A tiny slit nicked through each shell
keeps nuts from exploding
when heat claims moisture within.

I pull each pod from the fire,
throw casings into snow
where they sink like lumps of ore
melting into bottomless shafts.

In one of his few moves
toward intimacy
my father looks into my eyes
to tell me
my grandfather came to this country
to crawl through coal mines
until the Depression bullied him back to Italy.
Years later, he returned
saddled with family and English
broken as the bone
china packed inside his trunk
for a third passage through the pitch and swell
of fierce Atlantic.

His resilience
became my father's resilience. And later,
my own—the way I shut down in chaos, balk
at authority, and yearn for a place to root,
for my real life to begin.

Gifts

Six days a week
Dad works for another Italian, richest in the county.
Asphalt. Concrete. After land is pillaged
they roll in and pave, pour the foundation.
Contracts for schools, offices, strip malls
springing up.

Electrician by trade, my father installs power.
They return to me, his calloused hands
bandaged in gauze like white boxing gloves,
burns blackening his skin. The odor like stray dogs,
the stench at the landfill.

Crates of fruit, bottles of scotch,
turkeys the size of infants
arriving like orphans at our door.
Dad doing a little jig in the foyer as if fireworks
ignite at his feet.

I believed these gifts really fell off the truck
wondering why those so grateful to my father
waited for objects to drop from six-wheeler beds
instead of buying a present so they could boast
dat's-a lot a money, whataya gon' do?
Capisci?

like the men in my family usually say
when things cost so much.

TORRONE
Italian Nougat

Oil two 8 × 8 inch cake pans.

Toast and set aside

> 2 ⅓ CUPS WHOLE UNBLANCHED HAZEL NUTS

Place in top of double boiler over boiling water and stir with a wooden spoon for one hour

> 1 CUP OF HONEY

Remove honey from heat.

Beat until stiff peaks are formed

> 2 EGG WHITES

Add beaten egg whites to honey, 1 tablespoon at a time, beating well with wooden spoon after each addition. Set aside.

Combine in a skillet

> 1 CUP SUGAR
> 2 TABLESPOONS WATER

Bring to boiling over medium heat and cook, stirring occasionally, until caramelized.

Add caramelized sugar to honey mixture, a tablespoon at a time, mixing well after each addition.

Remove mixture to heavy saucepan. Stirring constantly, cook over direct heat until a small amount forms a soft ball in cold water. Remove from heat while testing. Add, all at once,

> HAZEL NUTS AND
> 2 CUPS WHOLE UNBLANCHED ALMONDS

Mix well and quickly pour into prepared pans.

Torrone

By the time Cannoli comes, pastry shells
gorged with ricotta and cream,
the children edge off their chairs,
shuffle between couch and kitchen
craving both sugar and sleep.

The women sip Strega, sweeter than sherry,
sit long enough to talk
about something other than food, food
and compliments lavished on food.

Torrone, caramelized nougats
wrapped in a tiny blue box,
adorned with scenes of Italy
and castles I told friends
my family lived in.

I thought my blonde schoolmates had something
I needed, that lies helped me fit in
though each untruth I shouldered
like air in a room
when you can no longer breathe:
In Venice, my father sculled a gondola
to the tower of "pizza"
cathedral-high, leaning farther and farther

Cool 20 minutes.

Cut nougat into pieces and wrap in waxed paper.

➤ ABOUT THIRTY-TWO I × 2 INCH PIECES ➤

till it fell. The vineyard you see
weaving along a village, the village
along a cobble street... it leads
to Uncle Mario's villa
bigger than Rockefella's!

CANNOLI

Set out 6 6-inch aluminum tubes (about ¾ inch in diameter)

It is said that in many Italian homes a thin broomstick is quickly converted to Cannoli "tubes" by cutting the broomstick into 6 inch lengths and scrubbing until smooth.

Filling

Combine and beat until smooth

> 3 CUPS RICOTTA CHEESE
> 1¼ CUPS SUGAR
> 2 TEASPOON VANILLA EXTRACT

Stir in thoroughly

> ½ CUP SEMI-SWEET CHOCOLATE PIECES

Place mixture in refrigerator to chill.

Shells

Sift together into a bowl

> 3 CUPS FLOUR
> ¼ CUP SUGAR
> 1 TEASPOON CINNAMON
> ¼ TEASPOON SALT

Cut in with pastry blender until pieces are size of small peas

> 3 TABLESPOONS SHORTENING

Stir in

2 EGGS, WELL BEATEN

Blend in, a tablespoon at a time

2 TABLESPOONS WHILE VINEGAR
2 TABLESPOONS COLD WATER

Turn dough onto a lightly floured surface and knead. Wrap in waxed paper and chill in refrigerator for 30 minutes.

Set out deep saucepan or electric deep-frying pan and heat fat to 360° F.

From stiff cardboard, cut an oval pattern (6 inches × 4½ inches).

Finely chop and set aside

½ CUP PISTACHIO NUTS

Roll chilled dough ⅛ inch thick on floured surface. With cardboard pattern and pastry cutter, cut ovals from dough. Wrap dough loosely around tubes. Seal edges by brushing with

EGG WHITE, SLIGHTLY BEATEN

Press edges together to seal.

Fry only as many Cannoli shells as will float uncrowded one layer deep in the fat. Fry about 8 minutes or until golden brown, turning occasionally. Drain fat onto absorbent paper towels.

Cool slightly and remove tubes. Cool completely.

To serve, fill pastry tubes with ricotta filling. Sprinkle ends of Cannoli with chopped nuts and dust shells with sifted confectioners' sugar.

⮞ ABOUT FIFTEEN CANNOLI ⮜

ABOUT THE AUTHOR

MARY LOU SANELLI was raised in Connecticut, educated in Boston, and now lives in Port Townsend, a coastal village located on Washington state's Olympic Peninsula, as well as in Seattle's downtown Belltown district. This is her fifth collection of poetry. Her poems have been published widely. Her poetic essays can be heard as commentary on KUOW Radio, a Seattle-based NPR station, and can be read in Port Townsend's newspaper, *The Leader*, in her column "A Writer's Notebook." She presents her work and teaches writing workshops throughout the country.

ACKNOWLEDGMENTS

Poems in this collection have previously appeared in:

Pontoon, Floating Bridge Press, "Pasta Fagioli"

The Temple, "Veal Scaloppine," "Manicotti," "Finocchio"

Art Access, "Frutta"

Arnazella Literary Arts Magazine, "Polenta"

Missing Spoke Press, Anthology, "Chestnuts"

Raven Chronicles, Southsound Edition, "Sliced Meat & Bread"

Slipstream, "Antipasto"

National League of American Pen Women, A 2000 Memorial Award, "Minestrone"

I wish to thank:

The Culinary Arts Institute of Chicago for their expertise

Jack Estes, my editor and publisher, for believing in me

My mother's recipes and memory...

HOW OUR PRESS GOT ITS NAME

from Pleasure Boat Studio, an essay written by Ouyang Xiu,
Song Dynasty poet, essayist, and scholar
(January 25, 1043)

"If one is not anxious for profit, even at the risk of danger, or is not convicted of a crime and forced to embark; rather, if one has a favorable breeze and gentle seas and is able to rest comfortably on a pillow and mat, sailing several hundred miles in a single day, then is boat travel not enjoyable? Of course, I have no time for such diversions. But since 'pleasure boat' is the designation of boats used for such pastimes, I have now adopted it as the name of my studio. Is there anything wrong with that?"

Translated by Ronald Egan